window

dressing

great outlooks: rooms with new views

window dressing

Stewart and Sally Walton

southwater

This edition is published by Southwater

Distributed in the UK by
The Manning Partnership
251–253 London Road East
Batheaston
Bath BA1 7RL
tel. 01225 852 727
fax 01225 852 852

Published in the USA by
Anness Publishing Inc.
27 West 20th Street
Suite 504
New York
NY 10011
fax 212 807 6813

Distributed in Canada by
General Publishing
895 Don Mills Road
400–402 Park Centre
Toronto, Ontario M3C 1W3
tel. 416 445 3333
fax 416 445 5991

Distributed in Australia by
Sandstone Publishing
Unit 1, 360 Norton Street
Leichhardt
New South Wales 2040
tel. 02 9560 7888
fax 02 9560 7488

Southwater is an imprint of Anness Publishing Limited
Hermes House, 88–89 Blackfriars Road, London SE1 8HA
tel. 020 7401 2077; fax 020 7633 9499

© Anness Publishing Limited 1996, 2002

Publisher: Joanna Lorenz
Senior Editor: Lindsay Porter
Photographer: Graham Rae
Stylist: Catherine Tully
Designer: Caroline Reeves

1 3 5 7 9 10 8 6 4 2

CONTENTS

INTRODUCTION

Basement, casement, balcony or bedsit – whatever the style, you're bound to find something

in this book to revolutionize your window. So, throw away those plastic hooks and tracks,

invest in a staple gun and some crafty fixings, and follow the step-by-step instructions to

show you where to look, what to get and how to bring your windows into focus.

You may never look in the curtain department again, once you have been liberated into the

world of saris, stage sets and scrim. Your enthusiasm will carry you away from traditional

methods and styles towards the exciting freedom of experimental window dressing.

Many of the projects in this book were inspired by looking at familiar materials in a new

light, such as using grass beach mats for blinds. There are all kinds of materials that can

make the leap from their practical everyday uses to decorative and original ones. There are

projects here to suit all tastes, and once you start thinking along these new

lines you are bound to come up with your own ideas as well.

So, shake off curtaining conventions and take a fresh look at the windows

around your home – who can tell what creations lie ahead?

USING COLOUR

If you are starting from scratch, with bare walls and no furniture, then you almost have free range as far as window dressing colour goes. For some, total freedom can be daunting, so if you have an existing carpet or soft furnishing fabric, take this as a starting point when making your fabric colour choice.

The best way to choose colour is to do it on site, with the windows and the rest of your belongings around you. Have a look through glossy magazines, books about art, travel, style, food, gardens – anything where you see combinations of colours that appeal to you. This should be fun and not a serious chore, so feel free to draw inspiration from whatever appeals to you. It is easy to become bewildered by choice when looking through fabrics in a store, so allow yourself time to consider other options.

Bear in mind that light affects the way colour performs. Colours that look stunning in Mexico cannot be expected to look the same in Northern Europe. There is a good reason why Scandinavian interiors favour pale yellow and blue-grey – the natural light is soft. In Mexico, the brilliant sunshine overpowers any colour that is not strong and vibrant and has a harmonizing effect on bright colours.

If this all sounds far too technical, remember that your personal preference is the most important of all, so go with your instincts. There are so many reasons why we like or dislike a colour, so even if purple is the most fashionable colour of the moment but you find it depressing, avoid it at all costs. Beauty is in the eye of the beholder, and one person's boring beige is another's delicious oatmeal. If you like the natural look, consider earthy reds, oranges and browns that have been dyed with natural pigments – they are warm and restful and look good with ethnic trimmings and accessories.

If you have a row of windows in a room, think of using the same fabric in a combination of colours. Hot-pink roller blinds can be set back into the window frame, with cobalt-blue muslin draped from a rail in front. Black and white are the ultimate contrast – use them with primary colours for a modernist look, or with a single colour from the rest of the room to knit the scheme together. The beauty of quick, inexpensive soft furnishings is that you can be bold with colour – and replace it later if you change your mind.

Above: These vibrant fabrics from the South of France have their origins in Indian textiles. Panels of unlikely colour combinations and patterns are mixed together in such a way that it is impossible to go wrong when mixing different prints together. There will always be a colour or pattern match somewhere.

Right: Strong primaries create a vibrant, idiosyncratic effect, reflected in the mismatching curtains at the window. Buy lengths of unbleached muslin and experiment with the colourful dyes available.

Below: Layers of orange and yellow at the window create a feeling of sunshine, even in the depths of winter. The light filtering through the fabric seems to infuse the room with warmth.

Above: The clever use of curtains and colours creates a cosy alcove. One panel of brilliant red hangs flush against the window, while a more generous drape hangs at a distance away from the glass, curtaining off the cushioned seats.

DRAPING EFFECTS

For traditional curtains, curtain header tape and tracks are used to make even drapes that can be pulled open or closed with convenient efficiency. The problem with this route is that it is expensive and time consuming. If you can afford it, and prefer the regular repeat folds that you get with a header tape, then enjoy the luxury of having your drapes professionally made and installed. If not, then read on!

The very simplest no-sew way to drape a window is to use a pair of sheets over a pole. Simply throw them over and pull the back and front to the same length. The two sheets should meet in the middle of the pole, and be pulled back to each side of the window. The idea can be adjusted to fit most windows, with any extra fabric arranged on the floor below for a touch of opulence.

Market stallholders will often give a special deal on a roll of fabric, which will provide enough material for elaborate drapes. There are some great "invisible" fabrics around, like suit lining, mattress ticking and calico, that are ideal for draping this way. Allow about three times the drop of your window and start in the middle at the top of the window. Arrange folds and swags, pleating as you staple. Be creative and don't feel as if you have to copy any "correct" way of draping the fabric – there are no set rules, just ideas and inspiration.

Above: Fine netting is hung in uneven lengths, crossed and tied at the sides of the windows.

Left: A narrow channel, just wide enough to hold a wooden dowel, has been sewn along the top of two white sheets. The fabric gathers into small pleats but it is not long enough to reach the floor. What might have been a disadvantage has been turned into a feature by the asymmetrical draping.

Above: White muslin has been elaborately draped to match the spirit of the hand-painted mural. The pole is a feature on its own, perfectly complementing the rise and fall of the drapery.

Left: A simple wooden pole is used here along with four plain white cotton sheets. Two sheets are draped over the pole on either side, providing enough fabric for really generous folds. The sheets are loosely tied on both sides at windowsill height, and are allowed to billow out on to the floor.

Above: This elegant window is draped with a single length of white sheeting. The wooden pole has been gilded and the fabric is loosely twisted around it, to fall on to the floor on both sides of the French windows. This only works if you don't actually need to draw the curtains, but it looks fabulous.

TIE-BACKS

Above: The rich, burnt-orange curtain is tied back with a sparkling twist of stranded beads. The colours pick up the light from the window and the colour from the fabric.

Tie-backs are rather like belts for curtains. They can be made of anything at all, from the most unobtrusive matching fabric, to a wacky garland of fake fruit. It is more the effect than the object which earns the name.

Conventional curtains are almost always enhanced by the extra draping that comes with tie-backs. The curtains can be partially drawn at the top, then pulled aside further down the window, to provide a more interesting shape for both the fabric and the framed space behind it.

The positioning of the tie-backs will change the shape and the visual proportions of the window. A short window will look longer if you use the tie-backs high up in the top third of the frame. This way the top is more like a draped pelmet and the curtains hang down as pleated columns on each side of the window. Positioned halfway down, the tie-backs give a waisted look to the window which is shortening – and useful in a tall room. Low tie-backs, just above or at windowsill level, look the most opulent. The fabric hangs in long pleats from the rail, draping low down into the tie-back then billowing out on to the floor below.

Instant curtain-makers will find tie-backs indispensable because curtains made with stapled pleats won't draw in the conventional way. They rely on tie-backs in a very practical sense, to admit daylight. If you are using a single curtain then a tie-back is essential. Make a feature of the asymmetrical drapery by using a stylish wrought iron bracket, fake flowers or a blowsy bow. Single curtains need to look like a deliberate choice and a bold tie-back will emphasize this.

Coloured, tasselled tie-backs can be bought, but the selection is limited so it may be worth making up some of your own. Collect braids, fringes, tassels, cord and ribbon that can be twisted, plaited and attached to lengths of fabric to create unique tie-backs. It is also worth looking out for chunky bead necklaces, strings of shells and unusual ethnic jewellery that would make great decorative features in themselves.

Above: Two sets of curtains hang at slightly different levels and they each have their own matching tie-back which loops over the same hook. The thick white rope is left plain for a subtle and stylish effect.

Top left: These tie-backs echo the effect of the twisted drape of the curtain. The casual knotting need only be done once, then secured with stitches. Attach half-rings at the back to meet the hooks on the wall.

Above: Simple bow tie-backs have been used quite high up the frame to give a lengthening effect to the window. They are freshly tied each day.

Above: The lightest of white voile has been pulled to the side to let the light in. The softness of the effect is further enhanced by using white voile roses as the tie-back.

HANGING TREATMENTS

Above: This iron curtain rail has a light, spherical finial, complemented by the integral iron rings. Small metal curtain clips link the fabric to the rail, while the fine pleats of the curtains add texture to the treatment.

Gone are the days when a standard pelmet covered the workings of your drapes – now we like to keep them on show and dress them up with a wonderful range of poles, rails and finials. Whether you favour brass, wood, wrought iron or chrome, you will find a vast range of styles on offer.

Practically speaking, you should consider two main elements when considering which treatment to use – the weight of the fabric and the state of the wall. A heavy fabric needs the security of strong brackets supporting the pole. You will need brackets at both ends, and possibly in the middle as well. It should stay level, not bow in the middle. Check the walls before you invest in that coveted iron pole – old plaster does not always conceal sound masonry and it will need to be rock solid. Always check both sides of the window – there just might be a concealed airbrick lurking behind the plaster, and one good fixing is not enough when suspending heavy ironwork.

If the fabric is light it may need no more than a wooden dowel and cup hooks. You can sew a channel along the top of the curtain and feed the fabric on to the dowel to cover it, then paint the small exposed ends. With this method, the hooks screw into the wooden window frame, so no drilling is needed. Curtain clips are another fantastic option for lightweight fabrics: you can adjust their spacing at a pinch to change the way they drape, and with ring attachments the curtains can still be drawn.

For thick, smooth fabric like denim, cotton duck, ticking or PVC-coated cotton you could consider large brass eyelets. These are supplied by camping and sailing shops, complete with a tool to insert them. They can be threaded with rope loops, large rings or threaded directly on to a rail.

Before investing in expensive wooden curtain poles, try customizing cheap ones from a builder's merchant. Use a colour that harmonizes with your fabric, or make the most of the special paint effect kits now available. Anything from verdigris through to a limed oak or gilded finish is possible.

Above: A simple twist at the end of the rail adds visual interest. The thick ticking fabric has been doubled to allow a firm eyelet fixing, and thick white rope is threaded through to make the curtain loop.

Above: This cheap and simple wooden rail has been painted to match the colour of the walls. It is held up on a brass bracket and the muslin is channelled at the top, to slide directly on to the pole.

Right: Contrasting fabric loops complement this plain curtain.

ALTERNATIVE TREATMENTS

Above: A stunning contemporary interpretation of a stained glass window is a one-off work of art. Experiment with glass paints, blending transparent colours to create unusual effects.

When planning a window treatment, consider the scheme as an integral part of the whole room. Consider the proportions of the window with respect to the rest of the room, the contents and the colours. Successful window dressing should be part of the whole rather than motivated by the whim of fashion.

Sometimes curtains are unnecessary and impractical – in a bathroom, for instance, or other small spaces – but there are so many other ways to treat a window that these need not be neglected, and in fact can become a design feature.

Wooden blinds are used in hot countries for practical reasons – they provide the cool darkness that is needed for the siesta hours as well as blocking out the early morning sun and providing security. Windows behind the shutters are often hung with fitted panels of embroidered crisp white cotton, fixed into the frame, rather than hung on the wall. Slatted shutters allow strips of bright light to enter the room, reminiscent of the tropics, whereas heart-shaped cut-outs give a Scandinavian feel to a room.

In the countryside or by the sea, windows often look out on wonderful views and are not overlooked by other buildings, so there is no need to obscure a view in or out. In this case the window can be treated as a frame for a painting – the treatment should enhance the view, not detract from it. One way to do this is to cut a shaped frame from plywood or MDF to fit inside the window frame. The frame can then be painted or covered with fabric. This is a good way of obscuring anything unsightly and is also useful for changing the architectural character of the window. If, for instance, replacement double-glazing panels have been fitted to your Gothic-style cottage, just cut Gothic arched window surrounds and fit them into the recess in front of the frames.

Stained glass panels are another option. They cast beautiful light and can be used to create a variety of effects. Victorian and Edwardian architects often used small squares of coloured glass to surround clear panels in skylights and stair windows, and it is still possible to buy these from demolition yards or architectural salvage companies. These can be simply propped against plain glass, or fitted by a glazier. A selection of small "suncatcher" glass panels can look good when hung together in a window – singly, however, they always look like an afterthought. As an alternative you could try creating your own. Glass paints come in brilliant transparent colours or try using them on a small paned window to create a patchwork of light.

Fabric such as fine muslin can be used as a fixed panel on windows that have no view and need obscuring. A stamped or stencilled pattern will break up the area and still allow the light to filter through. As a quick solution a panel could be fixed in place with a staple gun or drawing pins. You can also stamp or stencil directly on to the glass, and this is especially effective if the pattern you choose is a small repeat. Glass stencilled with a light coat of matt white car spray paint looks very much like etched or sandblasted glass.

Unsuitable curtains, often inherited from the previous occupants, can have a very depressing effect, so get rid of them. Arm yourself with a staple gun, plywood, glass paint – almost anything – and use the technique that suits you to make the windows your own.

Above: Strips of inexpensive plastic ribbon are fixed above and below the window, only partially obscuring the balcony outside. Such a treatment will provide some privacy, and makes an unusual statement.

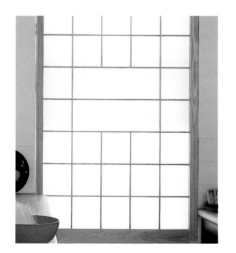

Left: A minimalist decor is carried through to the window treatment with this Japanese-style screen, which blocks the view while filtering light. See page 79 to make your own.

Above: The window frame surround has been cut in the shape of an Indian temple window. The paisley stamped muslin allows just enough light to filter through and the tassels complete the look.

WHITE MISCHIEF

Small details such as the curtain clips in this project make the important difference between an obvious and an elegant solution to curtain hanging. The white muslin lawn is a generously long piece, folded in half, allowing a drop 1¹/₂ times the length of the window – it really is a very simple, yet elegant example of window dressing! Small brass curtain clips fit over the rail and catch the muslin along the fold.

YOU WILL NEED

- dowel, window width
- woodstain
- kitchen cloth
- drill
- wallplugs and nails
- hammer
- 7 curtain clips
- white muslin lawn
- wooden spear or a garden implement

1 Stain a length of dowel by shaking woodstain on to a cloth and rubbing the dowel with it.

2 Drill two holes either side of the window in the wall and insert the wallplugs. Bang in the nails.

3 Clip the muslin along the fold, leaving an equal distance between the clips. Thread the rings on to the dowel and place the dowel over the nails.

4 Spread the rings along the dowel so that the muslin falls in even drapes.

5 Knot the front drop of muslin on to the end of the spear and prop this across the window.

18

ORANGE BOX BLIND

Greengrocers are used to supplying raw materials to their customers, but they might be a little surprised when you ask them for their wooden boxes rather than their apples and pears! Get hold of some of their orange boxes if you can, as the thin wooden planks make ideal and original slats for blinds.

These wooden blinds work best on a small, permanently obscurable window, such as the toilet. Although the blinds look Venetian, they don't actually pull up, but with a bit of perseverance and fiddly work, you could probably make them do that, too. Here the wood was left natural, but it could be stained any colour to complement an existing room scheme.

YOU WILL NEED

- ◆ orange boxes
- ◆ pliers
- ◆ sharp knife
- ◆ medium- and fine-grade sandpaper
- ◆ ruler
- ◆ pencil
- ◆ drill
- ◆ string
- ◆ scissors
- ◆ 2 chunky garage hooks

1 Pull the orange boxes apart and select the most interesting parts from the longest sides. Remove any wire staples with pliers.

2 Split some of the planks so that the slats are not all the same size. The final effect is more successful if the pieces are intentionally irregular.

3 Shave off some of the wood to add character to the finished blind.

4 Use medium- and fine-grade sandpaper to smooth the wood and round off the edges.

6 Drill through the positions you have marked. The holes should be big enough to take the string through twice, but no bigger.

8 Loop the string back over the slat and thread it through the hole a second time.

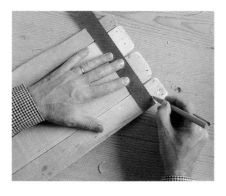

5 Place the slats side by side so that the edges line up. Mark a point 5cm/2in from each end and 3cm/1¼in from the bottom long edge. Although the slats are different widths, the holes need to be drilled through a point that lines up on the front of the blind.

7 Begin threading the string through the blind. Go through from the back and pull a long length, about twice the drop of the window. It will need to thread all the way down the blind.

9 Take the string up through the second slat. Continue as you did with the first, looping it around and through each slat twice, working all the way down the slats. ⟶

10 When you get to the last slat, tie the string in a double knot and cut it off. Repeat this process on the other side. This is what the blind will look like from the "working side".

11 Turn the blind round as shown to hang it up so you only see the string entering and leaving each slat. Screw two hooks up into the window frame and hang up the blind.

Above: The blind is simply hung from two garage hooks. Without a blind mechanism it cannot be raised or lowered in the traditional way, so it is best suited for a private area that does not require much natural light.

Right: The finished blind has an appealingly informal quality, reminiscent of wooden beach huts. Larger wooden crates, such as those used for shipping furniture, are made from thicker planks of wood, and they may not be suitable for this kind of window treatment.

NO-PROBLEM LINKS

What lengths will you go to for a bargain? If you find the fabric of your dreams in the remnant bin, but it's just that bit too short for your window, it's no longer a problem. Use curtain rings to connect the different lengths of fabric you have found – you can use as many as you need for the drop. Nobody will ever suspect that the linked effect was anything other than a deliberate design decision.

YOU WILL NEED

♦ drill

♦ spirit level

♦ wallplugs and screws

♦ screwdriver

♦ metal curtain rail and fixings

♦ assorted lengths of remnant fabrics

♦ iron-on hem fix (such as Wundaweb)

♦ iron

♦ needle and matching sewing thread

♦ split curtain rings

1 Attach the rail fixings above the window. Check with a spirit level before you screw them to the wall. Assemble the curtain rail and fixings.

2 Seam all the rough edges of the fabric, either with iron-on hem fix or by hand. Sew small split rings along the top edge of the curtain to link into the rail rings. Sew rings in the same positions along the bottom.

3 Line the curtain up with the next piece of fabric and mark the positions for attaching the rings. Make sure they line up with the first curtain if you have a geometric or striped pattern. Sew the rings to the other curtain along the whole width, then hang in place.

Above: The curtains can be linked with single rings, split rings or interconnecting rings like these.

RAINBOW STREAMERS

This really must be the quickest, cheapest and brightest way to deal with a bare kitchen window. All you need to do is buy an insect blind – those door-length, multi-coloured plastic strips. Then screw two cup hooks into the window frame to hold the rail and get your scissors out for a trim! The one in this project is V-shaped, but zig-zags, rippling waves, castellations or even asymmetrical designs are equally possible.

YOU WILL NEED

- ♦ wooden rail
- ♦ 2 cup hooks
- ♦ ruler
- ♦ pen
- ♦ door-size insect blind
- ♦ scissors

1 Place the rail along the top of the window and position the cup hooks so that the strips will hang over the whole width of the window.

2 Measure the windowsill to find the mid-point and make a small mark. This is where the blind will touch.

3 Place the ruler on a slant between the mark and the point you want the side drop to reach. Measure and mark the same point on the other side of the window frame.

4 Hang the insect blind on the rail and position it on the hooks, then hold the ruler up against it, between the two pen marks. Cut the strips along the top of the ruler.

BIJOU BOUDOIR

Ballroom dancers, bad-taste rockers, brides and prima ballerinas all love it – netting has that star quality that windows sometimes need! You can cut, pleat, layer, scrunch and bunch it – there is nothing to sew and it is so light that many lengths can hang from a single strand of plastic-coated sprung wire.

Netting comes in all sorts of colours and the idea from this project could easily be translated into a stunning party window in dramatic purple or scarlet and black. Tie the netting back with feather boas, strings of pearls or even diamanté dog collars to make this the most glamorous window this side of Cannes.

YOU WILL NEED
- ♦ pliers
- ♦ 4 eyelet hooks
- ♦ 2 lengths of plastic-coated sprung wire, window width
- ♦ 4 metres/4 yards each pink and white netting
- ♦ scissors
- ♦ fine wire
- ♦ feather boa
- ♦ fake pearl strands

2 Loop the eyelet on the wire through the hooks and stretch the wire taut across the window.

1 Screw in an eyelet hook either side of the window recess.

3 Repeat the process, positioning the second wire about 8cm/3in in front of the first (this distance will be dictated by the depth of your window recess).

4 Feed half the length of the pink netting over the back wire and pull it into shape to make a double layer.

6 Hang another layer of pink netting over the front wire.

8 Cut long strips of netting and scrunch them into rosettes. Tuck them between the wires. You will find that the netting is very easy to scrunch into good shapes. Pleat up the semi-circular pelmet, adding folds and creases along the wire as you go. ⟶

5 Feed the length of the white netting over the back wire, next to the pink netting and pull it into shape as before.

7 Cut out a large circle of pink netting to make the pelmet and fold this over the front wire to create a semi-circle.

Right: The finished effect is extravagant, with a touch of humour. When you want to clean the netting it is just as quick to take down as it was to assemble.

9 Make big white rosettes to go into the corners by scrunching up the white netting. Tuck them into the wire to secure and smooth them out to make a pleasing shape.

11 Drape the fake pearls from the centre of the front wire and tie up the ends.

Below: One of the great advantages of netting is that it is easy to handle, and is quite forgiving. If you don't like the first shape you have made, smooth it out and scrunch it up again. These rosettes are simply tucked between the front and back.

10 Twist the fine wire into connecting rings and use them to attach the boa along the curve of the pelmet.

RIBBONS AND LACE

Make the most of a beautiful piece of sari fabric or lace panel by displaying it in a window so that the light shines through. A few hand-stitched lengths of ribbon will allow you to tie back the fabric to reveal as much or as little of the window as you like. As the main fabric is very light, hang white muslin behind it for extra privacy.

YOU WILL NEED
♦ muslin, 1½ x window width
♦ iron-on hem fix (such as Wundaweb)
♦ iron
♦ white tape
♦ needle and white sewing thread
♦ dowel, window width
♦ 2 cup hooks
♦ scissors
♦ white or cream linen or satin ribbon
♦ sari fabric or antique lace panel

1 Finish off the seams on the muslin with iron-on hem fix, then sew lengths of white tape along the top to tie the muslin to the dowel. Screw the hooks into the window frame and hang up the dowel rail. Tie the curtain on to the rail.

2 Cut the ribbon into eight 25cm/10in lengths and stitch four along the top edge of the sari fabric or lace panel. Stitch the others at intervals along the sides – there is no set rule here and a lot will depend on the size of the panel and the parts that you want to show off. You can also hide any defects when you tie them up in this way.

3 Tie the top ribbons to the rail using simple bows. Arrange them along the rail so that the fabric drapes in the most appealing way.

4 Tie up sections of the panel using the side ribbons. Experiment with different combinations, standing back from the window to check your adjustments until you are happy.

WIRED-UP WINDOW

This is a quirky project for people who see the window as a frame to be filled, but not necessarily frilled! A selection of crisp Irish linen tea towels, linen scrim window cloths, dusters and oven gloves are arranged on a wire framework of tracks and hangers for a practical and stylish window treatment in the kitchen. Yachting chandlers sell good wire with all kinds of interesting bits and pieces for fastening and tightening up. Follow the steps here for an explanation on how to use them.

Look at this window treatment as a moveable feast and re-position the key elements every now and again to create a new design at no extra cost.

YOU WILL NEED

♦ rigging wire, 2 x window width; 1 x ½ window length plus 30cm/12in

♦ 2 wire grips

♦ 2 DIY rigging thimbles

♦ hammer

♦ pliers

♦ 2 deck eyes with pulleys

♦ bradawl

♦ 2 fixed deck eyes

♦ rigging screw (tension adjuster)

♦ connecting rings (key-ring style), various sizes

♦ wire coat hangers

♦ iron

♦ selection of new linen tea towels, dusters, cloths and oven gloves

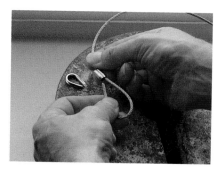

1 To make the rigging, thread the rigging wire through the wire grip to form a loop with the end.

2 Place the thimble inside the loop and pull the wire tight, so it fits snugly round the thimble. Place it on a hard surface and bang the grip closed with a hammer.

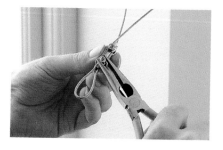

3 Loosen the screw on the thimbles and thread the wire through. Tighten the screw to hold the wire firmly – pliers will make it more secure.

4 Cut off the excess wire at the point where it enters the thimble.

5 Loop the thimble fitting over a deck eye, then hold it in position on the window frame using a bradawl to make holes for the screws. Screw the deck eye into the frame.

6 Thread the wire through one of the pulleys and screw this into the frame opposite the first fixing.

7 Thread the wire through the second pulley and screw this into the frame halfway down the side of the window.

8 Attach a thimble to the end of the shorter length of wire. Loop this through a deck eye and screw it into the frame halfway down the side of the window – opposite the last pulley.

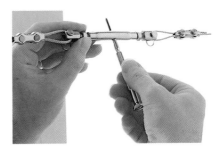

9 Attach an adjustable wire grip so that it can join on to each end of the rigging screw. Because of the nature of a rigging screw, you will be able to make minor adjustments to centralize it, but aim to cut the wire as accurately as possible to begin with. Twist the rigging screw to increase the tension.

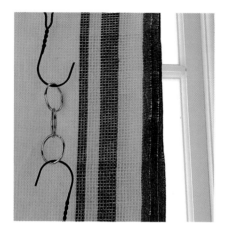

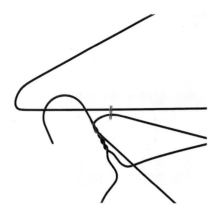

Right: The finished arrangement provides only a small degree of privacy, so is best suited to a kitchen, or a window with frosted glass. The large hanger came from a clothing shop, and completes the look of controlled eccentricity.

10 To assemble the arrangement, use connecting rings to link the coat hangers together.

12 To make further variations of the linked coat hangers, experiment with them until you are really pleased with the arrangement.

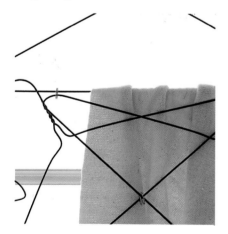

11 You could also make up "cat's cradle" shapes by interlinking hangers. Always reinforce the links with rings to make them more secure.

13 Finally, iron the tea towels and fold them with the dusters, oven gloves and cloths over the hangers.

EASTERN PROMISE

This window seat recess was given a touch of Eastern mystery by layering fine sari lengths behind each other to build up to a rich colour. The light picks up the gold embroidered flecks and braids, and the star lantern between the curtains casts its own magic spell. If you have never been in a sari shop, you will be awe-struck by the exquisitely patterned silks and voiles available.

YOU WILL NEED

♦ 7 sari lengths (you could have fewer)
♦ braid, 7 metres/7 yards plus width of each sari for braid edging
♦ iron-on hem fix (such as Wundaweb)
♦ iron
♦ needle and matching sewing thread
♦ wooden curtain rail
♦ drill
♦ wallplugs and hooks
♦ wrought iron curtain rail

1 If the saris do not have braid edges, add them with iron-on hem fix. Cut the remaining braid into 14cm/5½in lengths to make seven loops along the top of each sari. Space them at equal distances and use small slip stitches to secure them.

2 Put the wooden curtain rail through all the loops of three of the saris and fix the rail into the recess with hooks. Hang the iron rail on the outer frame, and hang two saris (here red and yellow) on the left of the rail by threading their loops alternately so that one hangs in front. Hang the two other saris on the right by threading the same way.

3 Separate the red and yellow saris, holding one in each hand about halfway down their length.

4 Wrap the yellow one round the red one and knot them together. Arrange the folds of the knot so that the fabric tumbles away and spills to the floor.

AFRICAN DAYS

Kenyan cloths are gorgeously rich and vibrant. The patterns and colours are brilliant and there is no need to hem, stitch or gather them. Just run a washing line across the window and peg the cloth on to it – use colour co-ordinated pegs and line to pull the whole look together. You won't be able to draw this curtain, but keep an extra peg or two handy so you can use them to hold the cloth back and let the sunshine in.

YOU WILL NEED

- ♦ 2 cup hooks or eyelets
- ♦ plastic-coated washing line
- ♦ multi-coloured plastic pegs
- ♦ African cloth panel

1 Screw the hooks into the wall (or window frame) at an equal distance from the window.

2 Loop the washing line around the hooks and tie a knot.

3 Peg the cloth to the line, gathering it up a bit for the first and last pegs to add weight around the edges.

4 Bundle up the excess line on one side and tie it in a knot. Let this hang down instead of cutting it off neatly – who knows when you may need a washing line?

DRAWING-ROOM SECRETS

Just because you invest heavily in some great curtain fabric, you should not feel committed to spending at least as much again on having it made up. This really is a completely no-sew curtain and pelmet idea that could easily pass for the work of a true professional!

To work out how much material you need, just measure the drop and allow three times that length. The seams are all iron-on and the rest is done with a staple gun and string – it's hard to imagine that such an elegant draped pelmet could be put together without sewing a stitch. Follow the steps to discover the hidden secrets that lie behind this drawing-room window.

YOU WILL NEED
- striped fabric
- scissors
- iron-on hem fix (such as Wundaweb) or double-sided carpet tape
- iron
- 2 wooden battens, window width plus 30cm/12in each side
- spirit level
- drill
- wallplugs and screws
- screwdriver
- staple gun
- string

1 Divide the fabric into three equal lengths, two for the curtains and one for the pelmet. Turn over the seams on both ends of the pelmet and one end of each of the curtains. Fix the seams with iron-on hem fix, or carpet tape if the fabric is very heavy.

2 Fix the thin side of one of the battens to the wall so that the ends overlap the window equally – use a spirit level to check the position. Screw the other length on to it at a right angle.

3 Starting at one end, staple the edge of one curtain to the front of the batten. Use the staple gun on its side so that the staples are inserted vertically – this places less stress on the fabric and it creates neater pleats.

4 Supporting the weight of the fabric, move to the middle of the window and staple the other corner of the curtain. It is now attached at both ends, with most of the fabric hanging loose in the middle. To make the pleats, hold the curtain away from the window and find the middle. Staple this to the middle of the batten.

5 Find the middle of the two loose sections and staple them to the middle of the timber. Keep sub-dividing the batten and the fabric until you have reached the pleat width you want. Repeat the process for the other curtain so it matches.

6 Fold the fabric for the pelmet in half lengthways and line this up with the centre of the window. You will staple along one long edge, to the top of the batten, close into the wall. Start stapling at the centre and move outwards, then return to the centre and go in the other direction. Lift the side drops of the pelmet and gather up the fabric at the corners. Put a row of staples underneath the gather so that the stripes of the pelmet line up with the curtain stripes below.

7 Bunch up the fabric at each corner and tie it with string. Be aware of the way the fabric folds at this stage – you may need to practise folding and tying a few times until you achieve the desired effect.

8 Staple the string to the batten – it won't show, so use as many staples as you like to make it secure.

9 Tie another piece of string around the drop of the pelmet, about 30cm/12in down. Tie it tightly, leaving enough string to allow you to tie another knot to raise this section to the top corner.

10 Pull the fabric up to the corner and tie the string ends tightly around the first knot. Push the knots inside the remaining fabric to puff the front out. If necessary, add staples to hold this in place along the top of the batten. Finally, arrange the pleats and folds.

Right: The completed curtain provides a fitting framework for a window seat or other large, deeply recessed window. The wire tie-back – on one curtain only – adds a contemporary touch. Gold cord with tasselled ends could also be used, but would create a different effect.

Below: Simply by draping, stapling and tying, you can create a Neo-Classical style swagged pelmet.

ROBINSON CRUSOE BLINDS

This is one of the most inexpensive and stylish blind solutions ever: it involves two grass beach mats, three cup hooks, a length of rope and some brass paper fasteners. The beach mats are made with coloured tape binding, and as they are extremely lightweight, they can be rolled up by hand and tied with rope. Measure your window carefully – the mats come in one width only, so are not suitable for all windows.

YOU WILL NEED

- ♦ bradawl
- ♦ 3 cup hooks
- ♦ 2 grass beach mats
- ♦ paper fasteners
- ♦ rope
- ♦ scissors

1 Make three holes with a bradawl, one either side and one in the middle of the window recess. Screw in the cup hooks.

2 Make a channel for the rope at the top of the blind by folding over the mat 4cm/1½in and securing with a row of paper fasteners, pushed through and folded back.

3 Knot the rope on to one of the cup hooks, leaving a tail hanging about a third of the way down the window. Thread the rope through the blind and pull it tight before knotting it on to the middle hook. Cut the rope the same length as before.

4 Cut a length of rope twice the length of the window drop and knot it in the middle, on to the middle hook. Roll up the blind and tie the rope to hold it at the required height. Repeat for the second blind.

PURPLE PLAYROOM

These lush purple felt drapes will knock the socks off most playroom curtains! They were inspired by the little boxes of felt shapes that children play with on boards. These are readily available in a wide range of topics – farms, fairies and fish, to name but a few. As you have to press out the pre-cut shapes from the background nowadays, you get a great negative shape as well as your motifs. Use the background on the pelmet and the tie-backs and decorate the curtains with your chosen motifs. Use different shapes and colours for a more adult curtain.

YOU WILL NEED

- wooden batten, 5 x 2.5cm/2 x 1in thick
- spirit level
- drill
- wallplugs and screws
- screwdriver
- pinking shears
- deep purple felt, 2 metres/2 yards wide x the drop plus 40cm/16in
- commercial pre-cut felt shapes
- fabric glue
- chalk
- drawing pins
- staple gun (optional)

1 Fix the batten up above the window, extending at least 20cm/8in beyond the frame on both sides. Check the position with a spirit level before you screw it to the wall.

2 Use pinking shears to cut out two strips of curtain felt the width of the fabric and 2cm/¾in deeper than the pre-cut felt squares. These will be stuck along the edge of the pelmet.

3 Apply fabric glue to the back of the pre-cut felt backgrounds, in key points, then spread it out to the edges.

4 Stick different coloured squares along the length of the strips, taking into account the spacing needed for the gathers. Apply fabric glue to the back of both strips and stick them on the wrong side of the top edge of the curtain lengths. (Both sides of the curtain fabric are the same, but the strips will be on the undecorated side.)

6 Judge the width of the possible pleating from the width of the window and the width of your fabric. Working with one curtain at a time, pin a few secure pleats on one side.

7 Continue pleating and securing with drawing pins (or a staple gun, if you prefer) until you complete the curtain. Repeat this process for the other curtain. As you are using pins, you will be able to check the pleats and adjust them as you go. ⟶

5 On the right side of the curtain, draw a chalk line 40cm/16in down from the top. Pin the two curtain edges to meet in the centre of the batten, holding the top 40cm/16in above it. Pin the outside edges to each end of the batten.

Left: A variety of felt shapes and colours which can be used to decorate the curtain and pelmet.

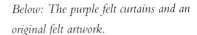

Right: The curtains can be left hanging freely, or held back with a simple tie-back. The thickness of the felt provides warmth in the winter. The same simple method for the pleats and pelmet can be used in all weights of fabric, but is more successful with heavier fabrics.

8 When the pleating is complete, allow the pelmet to flop down over the pinning, and arrange the pleats to match those in the curtains.

10 If desired, make tie-backs in the same style as the pelmet.

Below: The purple felt curtains and an original felt artwork.

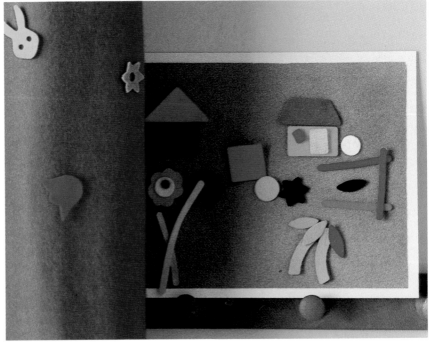

9 Arrange all the small felt shapes randomly on the curtains. They will cling to the felt without glue for a while – long enough for you to have some fun and move things around until you like the arrangement. For permanence, use fabric glue to keep them in place.

EGYPTIAN DREAM

A pair of cotton sheets makes the most wonderful drape and all the seams are perfectly finished. The bigger the sheets, the more luxurious the window will look — drapes should always be generous. Wooden pegs can be wedged into a piece of old wooden floorboarding — if you drill the holes at an angle, the fixing will be stronger as well as more decorative.

1 Using sharp scissors, cut the tape into six strips of equal length. These will be used to attach the sheets.

3 Drill six holes at equal distances along the floorboarding and wedge in the pegs. Drill a hole either end of the floorboarding and screw it into the wall, using a spirit level to check it is straight, and appropriate fixings to secure it.

YOU WILL NEED

- ◆ scissors
- ◆ cotton tape, 2½ metres/2½ yards
- ◆ 2 flat king-size cotton sheets
- ◆ needle and white sewing thread
- ◆ drill
- ◆ length of floorboarding or driftwood, window width plus 15cm/6in either side
- ◆ 6 old-fashioned wooden pegs
- ◆ spirit level
- ◆ wallplugs and screws
- ◆ screwdriver

2 Divide the width of each sheet top by three and use the divisions as points to attach the tapes. Fold each tape in half and use small stitches to sew them to the top of the sheet.

4 Tie the tapes to the pegs and arrange the drapes.

ARTIST'S STUDIO

This is the ideal way to cover a large studio window, and as canvas comes in so many sizes, you're bound to find a piece to fit your window. If you've never considered the possibility of becoming a painter, then this is a good way to start – curtains can be art!

Here, chalks were used to draw on to the canvas and change the flat panel into a boldly gathered backdrop. You could use this idea as your inspiration, or you could flick colours on it in Jackson Pollock style, or simply add a few minimalist squiggles. If your window receives a lot of light, you may want to suspend a builder's dust sheet in front of the window. This will provide a lining for the main curtain.

YOU WILL NEED

- ◆ canvas, 1½ x window width
- ◆ chalks or acrylic paints and paintbrush
- ◆ drill
- ◆ 4 chunky garage hooks
- ◆ screwdriver
- ◆ metal cleat
- ◆ rope
- ◆ double-sided carpet tape
- ◆ brass eyelets
- ◆ hammer

1 Draw, paint or print on to the canvas using whatever style or design you have chosen – the bolder the better, as the canvas will cover a large area.

2 Fix the chunky garage hooks into the wall above the window, at four equal intervals.

3 Screw the cleat to the wall, about halfway down the side of the window, then wind one end of the rope around it several times.

4 Take the long end of the rope up and through the hooks along the top.

5 Pull the rope taut and tie it on to the end hook. Then fix the seams and eyelets on to the canvas (see *No-Frills Navy* project).

6 Thread the rope through the first eyelet from behind, allowing about 16cm/6¼in between the hook and the eyelet. Then, leaving the same distance again, twist a loop in the rope and put it on the hook.

7 Take the rope down and through the back of the next eyelet, then up and over the back taut rope, which is now a rail for the rope to rest on.

8 When you reach the end of the curtain, take the rope through the last hook.

9 Take the rope straight down the side of the window and tie it on to the cleat.

10 Cut an extra length of rope and hook it over one of the top centre hooks so that one length falls to the front and the other to the back of the canvas. Gather the canvas up and get hold of both ends of the rope. Tie these together in a knot and leave the ends dangling free.

Above: The knot holding the curtain back from the window allows in the light.

Above: The knotted rope is a decorative element in its own right.

Above: Allow enough canvas to spill generously out on to the floor below.

Above: The natural colour of the canvas enhances the subtle colours of the design.

Right: The finished curtain provides a theatrical note in a modern interior. Accessories can be kept to a minimum with such a dramatic window treatment.

BUTTONED BLANKETS

These blankets were too brilliant to hide away in the bedroom so they were transformed into an attractive window treatment. They make effective draught excluders and are simply rigged up on a couple of towel rails. You need a solid wall for this idea as the blankets are quite weighty. The blankets are doubled over and held together with a row of large safety pins.

1 Fix the towel rails to the wall above the window by drilling holes and inserting wallplugs. As towel rails are not long enough to cover the whole width, hang them at different heights.

3 Stitch the buttons along the pelmet, just catching the first layer with a few stitches to secure the buttons, but without damaging the blanket.

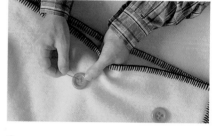

YOU WILL NEED

- ◆ 2 chrome towel rails
- ◆ drill
- ◆ wallplugs and extra-long screws
- ◆ screwdriver
- ◆ 2 colourful wool blankets
- ◆ 10 large coloured buttons, to contrast with blanket colours
- ◆ dressmakers' pins or double-sided tape
- ◆ needle and button thread or wool
- ◆ large safety pins or nappy pins

2 Fold both the blankets in half lengthways. Drape them over the curtain rails to create a 30cm/12in pelmet as shown. Take down the blankets. Decide upon the position of the buttons, by fixing them to the blankets with dressmakers' pins or double-sided tape.

4 Pin a row of safety pins about halfway down the pelmet, on the underside where the pins won't show. Hang the blankets back in their original position. Re-pin, so that each safety pin goes through the inside layer of the pelmet, and the outer layer of the curtain.

HULA-HULA WINDBREAK

Ordinary windbreaks used on the beach can be transformed into instant blinds. They come in a range of lengths with poles in pockets to divide the equal sections – just like a Roman blind, but bolder. All you have to do is saw off the extra bit of pole that goes into the sand and hang up the blind on a couple of plumbers' pipe fittings.

YOU WILL NEED

- ♦ windbreak, to fit window
- ♦ scissors
- ♦ stapler
- ♦ saw
- ♦ tape measure
- ♦ drill
- ♦ 2 wallplugs
- ♦ 2 plumbers' pipe fittings
- ♦ screwdriver
- ♦ flower garlands, elastic or rope
- ♦ string (optional)

1 If the drop of the blind is much too long for your window, then cut out the nylon mesh and make a new channel for the bottom pole. Fold over a seam, making sure the pole fits, and staple along the edge.

2 Saw off the excess pole, then measure the window and the top of the blind to find the position for the fixings. Drill holes and insert the wallplugs and plumbers' fittings.

3 Hang the blind, then loop the garlands, elastic or rope between the first and last poles. If the garlands are too long, tie them in divisions with string to shorten.

Above: The Hawaiian garland used to hold up the blind. To lower the blind, simply unhook the garland from the lowest pole.

WOVEN BLINDS

This coloured milliner's scrim is one of the new natural materials now available. It is stiff enough to hold its shape and be folded into sharp creases. Use this treatment for a window needing to be obscured from prying eyes while still allowing maximum light to penetrate the room. To make the most of their soft colours, the milliner's scrim has been interwoven.

YOU WILL NEED

♦ strips of milliner's scrim in 3 colours, 6cm/2½in wide

♦ scissors

♦ tape measure

♦ 2 broom handles

♦ staple gun

♦ stapler

♦ bradawl

♦ 2 plumbers' pipe fittings

♦ screwdriver

1 Cut strips of milliner's scrim to the length of the drop, plus 20cm/8in. Wrap a 10cm/4in strip around a broom handle and secure it with a staple gun. Leaving 3cm/1¼in gaps between each strip, continue fixing the strips along the broom handle with the staple gun. Finish with 9cm/3½in of bare wood at the end. Repeat this process to fix the ends of the strips to the second broom handle.

2 Cut the remaining two colours into strips that fit the width of the blind plus a 3cm/1¼in seam allowance each side. Weave these through the strips on the broom handles.

3 At each side, turn the seam over and crease it with your thumbnail, then staple the two strips together.

4 Use a bradawl to make two small holes either side of the underside of the top recess, then screw in the plumbers' fittings. Put the broom handle in position, then screw the front section of the fittings into position.

SCOTLAND THE BRAVE

Here is the perfect way to show off bright tartan wool rugs. Draped and pinned over a wooden rail, they will add a baronial touch to the plainest of windows. Tartan has quite a masculine feel and looks good alongside old leather cases and "practical" accessories. This window would suit a study or hallway with plain walls, contrasting with the richness of the tartan. Fix the curtain rail above the window, extending about 30cm/12in each side.

YOU WILL NEED

- ♦ wooden curtain rail
- ♦ spirit level
- ♦ drill
- ♦ wallplugs and screws
- ♦ screwdriver
- ♦ 3 different coloured tartan rugs
- ♦ 6 kilt pins

1 Fix the curtain rail as described in the introduction. Begin on the left with one corner of a rug. Take the corner over from the back and pin it about 30cm/12in down the rug.

2 Drape the second rug over the rail, also on the left, but arrange it so that the drape is more or less equal at the front and back. Lift it in places and pin it on to the first rug.

3 Drape the third tartan rug along the rest of the pole diagonally so that the fringed edge can be seen hanging down from the right corner. Lift sections of this rug and pin it in drapes by attaching it with kilt pins to the second rug.

4 Stand back and check the effect, then use any remaining pins to hold the rugs in place, making a feature of the fringing and the pins.

HESSIAN AND SCRIM BLINDS

The natural materials of hessian and linen scrim team up with bamboo canes to make this unusual Roman blind. Linen scrim is normally used for cleaning windows, and it has the reputation of being the ultimate glass polishing cloth – so it is on familiar but elevated ground here, having been promoted from cleaning to decorating. The blind obscures the window effectively at night and by day the sunlight streams through the scrim, making it appear almost transparent. The bamboo canes give the window a "potting shed" effect and the final detail of the ingenious pulley adds a Heath Robinson touch – not only does it look interesting, but it is also practical.

YOU WILL NEED

- ◆ hessian, to fit window
- ◆ scissors
- ◆ scrim, same size as hessian
- ◆ stapler
- ◆ iron-on hem fix (Wundaweb) and iron (optional)
- ◆ 6 bamboo canes
- ◆ tape measure
- ◆ saw
- ◆ needle and matching sewing thread
- ◆ 12 x 1cm/¾in brass rings
- ◆ 2 x 1cm/¾in hinged rings
- ◆ coat hangers
- ◆ pliers
- ◆ pencil
- ◆ thin card
- ◆ 4 empty wooden cotton reels
- ◆ 4 screws
- ◆ screwdriver
- ◆ washers (optional)
- ◆ string

1 Cut the hessian into four strips to make a border for the scrim. Working on the sides of the blind first, fold a strip of hessian down the length of either side of the scrim. This will form a border, enclosing the raw edges of the scrim. Staple the hessian and scrim together. If you want to use iron-on hem fix to strengthen the edges, leave a gap at the edge to insert some after the stapling.

2 Divide the length of the drop by six to calculate the position of the bamboo canes. Saw the bamboo canes to fit the width of the window. Insert the first cane in position by holding it with the ends pushed up into the hessian border and stapling either side of it to make a channel. Repeat this process on the other side. Position the next four canes in the same way, at equal intervals.

3 Fold the hessian over the scrim at the bottom, as you did with the side, with a bamboo cane along its bottom fold. Staple this in place. Repeat this process with the top edge.

4 If you are using iron-on hem fix, place it under the seam between the scrim and hessian and press it with a hot iron.

5 Trim off any overlapping hessian. You could insert some iron-on hem fix if the fabric frays.

6 Stitch a brass ring to every point at which the hessian and scrim meet on a bamboo strut, including the bottom strut. Take the needle right through the fabric so that the thread goes around the bamboo each time for a strong fixing. Sew the two hinged rings, in line with the others, either side of the blind top.

7 Cut five lengths of coat hanger wire from the longest part of the hanger – three lengths at 16cm/6¼in and two lengths at 26cm/10in.

8 Using the photograph as a guide, draw the shape to hold the reels on to a piece of card. Then bend the shorter pieces of wire to that shape so they will hold the reels to make a pulley.

9 Use the two longer lengths of wire to bend into simple U-shapes to hold the blind, as shown.

10 Screw the first reel into the top right corner – ensure that the screw heads are big enough, or add a washer to get a firm fixing. Align the loops of a second pulley and a wire to hold the blind. Fix both gadgets in place with the same screws. Screw the other reel and wire on the other side of the window, the same distance from the edge.

11 Open out the hinged ring and use it to clip the blind up in the window.

12 To thread the blind, start at the bottom and tie the string to the lowest ring. Thread up through the rings and over the pulleys on both sides of the blind. Thread both strings along the top, to the third pulley.

13 Tie the two strings together about 15cm/6in down from the corner pulley to prevent the blind from pulling up unevenly. Screw the last cotton reel into the wall for tying the string when you pull the blind.

MAGIC BEADS

Transparent beads don't block out the light or keep out the draughts, but when the sun catches them, they sparkle like jewels, and using them full-length on a small square window can turn a light source into something bright and magical.

YOU WILL NEED

- ◆ 2 wooden battens, window width plus 8–10cm/3–4in each side
- ◆ wood glue
- ◆ hammer
- ◆ panel pins
- ◆ ruler
- ◆ emulsion paint: black and white
- ◆ paintbrush
- ◆ drill
- ◆ coloured bead curtain, with fixings
- ◆ screwdriver
- ◆ wallplugs and screws
- ◆ spirit level
- ◆ small jewelled drawer knob

1 Make the pelmet by sticking one edge of a batten to the long edge of the other to form a right angle. Hammer in a few panel pins to secure it. Divide the length into equal sections and paint them alternately black and white.

2 Drill, then screw through the holes in the bead fixing strip to secure it underneath the top of the pelmet.

3 Drill, insert wallplugs and screw the pelmet in place above the window. Use a spirit level to check the position after attaching one side. Hang the lengths of beads along the fixing strip.

4 Drill a hole, insert a wallplug and screw in the drawer knob in position – level with the base of the window if it is small, or halfway down if you have got a larger window.

NO-FRILLS NAVY

No frills in this project! Block out the light with this crisp and stylish navy blue curtain.

Cotton duck is as heavy as denim but to add firmness and thickness to the top seams, you can use double-sided carpet tape to bond them together. This also means that you get a good fit with the large brass eyelets that are made for tent canvas and sails.

When you are buying your fabric, you will need to get about one and a half times the width of your window plus a seam allowance of 5cm/2in top and bottom to get perfect pleats like these. It is always a good idea to err on the generous side with curtaining, so stretch the budget rather than the fabric on this project!

YOU WILL NEED
- navy cotton duck
- double-sided carpet tape
- backing card
- ruler
- pencil
- hole punch
- hammer
- brass eyelets
- rigging wire, window width
- 2 wire rope grips
- 2 thimbles
- pliers
- drill
- 2 wallplugs and large hooks

2 Fold the top seam over the tape, smoothing as you go to ensure a crisp, wrinkle-free finish.

3 Place the curtain on a sheet of backing card. Using a ruler and a pencil, mark the positions for the holes at 20cm/8in intervals. Put the back part of the hole punch in position behind the fabric to make the first hole.

1 Stick a length of double-sided tape along the top of the fabric, one tape width in from the edge. Peel off the top paper.

4 Position the top part of the hole punch and bang it firmly with a hammer.

6 Fit the middle of the eyelet through the punched hole.

8 Position the tool provided with the eyelets and bang it firmly with a hammer. Continue positioning the eyelets at the marked intervals along the top of the curtain.

5 Place the back part of the eyelet in the back part of the hole punch.

7 Place the top half of the eyelet on top of the bottom half.

9 Thread the rigging wire through the wire grip to form a loop. Place the thimble inside the loop and pull the wire taut. Using a hammer on a hard surface, bang the wire grip closed.

Right: The clean lines of the finished curtain perfectly complement a modern decor. Nothing could be easier to draw back when more light is required – the eyelets slide smoothly along the rigging wire, and the pleats remain as crisp as ever.

10 You may find that a squeeze with a pair of pliers will be needed to close the wire grip fully.

12 Thread the other end through the wire grip as before, then attach it to a hook. Screw the hook into a pre-drilled and plugged hole. This will ensure even pleats.

11 Drill holes and fix one of the hooks in the window recess. Loop the rigging wire over it. Thread the curtains on to the rigging wire through the eyelets.

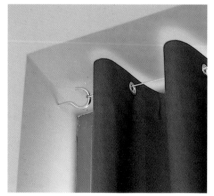

Above: The equal spacing of the eyelets ensures that the pleats ripple across the window in perfect symmetry.

MILLINER'S MADNESS

If you have ever felt like going right over the top with your home decorating, milliner's velvet must be the curtain choice for you! Milliner's velvet comes in gorgeous colours and it is great to work with. It is backed with paper and folds into the biggest cabbage roses and most luscious drapes imaginable.

YOU WILL NEED

♦ wooden batten, window width plus 10cm/4in either side

♦ spirit level

♦ drill

♦ wallplugs and screws

♦ screwdriver

♦ milliner's velvet in dark green and pink

♦ scissors

♦ staple gun

♦ tape measure

♦ 2 or more artificial cabbages on wire stems

1 Fix the batten up above the window. Check the position with a spirit level before you screw it to the wall.

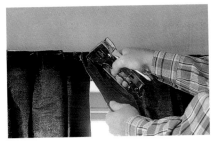

2 Cut the green velvet to the desired curtain length, then cut in half lengthways, and staple one corner of the fabric to the end of the batten. Staple the other corner to the middle of the batten. Staple the centre of the fabric midway between the two stapled ends. Continue pleating and stapling the fabric along the batten.

3 Repeat the pleating process with the other length of green velvet, taking care that the two curtains meet in the centre of the batten.

4 To make the pelmet, cut rectangular pieces of green velvet, roughly 1½ times the width of the window. Bunch them up and staple them into drapes across the top.

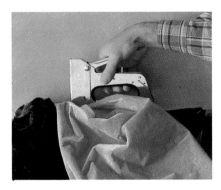

5 Divide the pink velvet into three equal pieces. Staple one end of velvet to the end of the pelmet, then scrunch into a large rose, by rolling the fabric around your fist several times. Secure the rose with as many staples as it takes, tucking in any rough edges. Repeat at the other end of the pelmet, then with the central rose.

7 Roll the curtain into a twist, then tuck it behind the cabbage.

8 Pull the cabbage tie-back in front of the curtain, then staple it in place at the back. Repeat with the other cabbage tie-back, tucking in additional pieces if desired.

6 Holding the curtain back, staple the wire stem of the artificial cabbage to the wall.

Left: The cabbage tie-backs are echoed in the pink velvet "cabbages" decorating the pelmet. This is definitely not a look for the shy or conservative.

JAPANESE SCREEN

This screen is the perfect treatment for a minimalist room scheme. The wooden screen lets you hide away from the outside world, yet still benefit from the light filtering through the window.

The screen is made from a simple wooden garden trellis, painted matt black, with heavyweight tracing paper stapled behind it. You can cut the trellis down to fit your window recess, but always do it to the nearest square so it keeps its balanced look. The tracing paper can be cut and stapled behind the struts so that it appears as one piece. So, follow the steps and add an instant oriental flavour to your room!

YOU WILL NEED

- ◆ garden trellis
- ◆ blackboard paint
- ◆ paintbrush
- ◆ heavyweight tracing paper
- ◆ staple gun
- ◆ craft knife
- ◆ red emulsion paint
- ◆ drill
- ◆ 2 eyelets
- ◆ tape measure
- ◆ wire coat hanger
- ◆ pliers
- ◆ 2 picture hooks

2 Staple sheets of tracing paper on to the back of the trellis.

3 If necessary, trim the tracing paper with a craft knife so that no overlaps or joins are visible from the front. It must look like a single sheet.

1 Paint the trellis black and leave to dry. Blackboard paint creates a perfectly matt finish, but other matt or gloss paints can be used.

4 For added interest, paint one square red and leave to dry.

6 Screw an eyelet into each hole.

Above: A single stem of orchids is highlighted against the diffused light from the screen.

Right: A garden trellis provides a clear framework for this screen. The secret to a professional finish lies in making sure none of the tracing paper sheets overlap at the back.

5 Drill a very fine hole in the top of the trellis, at the first strut in from each end.

7 Measure the length of the window to determine how long the hooks for hanging should be. The base of the screen should touch the window frame below. Cut two pieces of coat hanger wire to the correct length for the hooks, then hang the screen on these from picture rail hooks.

VICTORIAN STENCILLING

This idea originated from the etched glass windows of the Victorian era. You can easily achieve a frosted, etched look by using a stencil and car enamel paint on plain glass. The paint needs to be sprayed very lightly, so practise on some picture frame glass first to judge the effect. The stencil design is provided at the back of the book, but you could easily design your own. Look at examples of lace panels to get some inspiration.

YOU WILL NEED

♦ tape measure
♦ masking tape
♦ tracing paper
♦ stencil card
♦ pencil
♦ craft knife
♦ brown paper
♦ matt white car enamel spray

1 Measure the panes and mark the halfway points with masking tape. Trace and cut the stencil design in the back of the book from stencil card.

2 Tape the main stencil pattern in position, then use brown paper to mask off the surrounding area, at least 50cm/20in deep on all sides (the spray spreads more than you think).

3 Follow the paint manufacturer's instructions and shake the can for as long as needed, as this affects the fineness of the spray. Spray from a distance of at least 30cm/12in.

4 Depending on the dimensions of the window panes, there may be strips along the sides of the main panel that also need stencilling. This pattern has a border to fit around the edge – you may need to adapt it to fit your pane.

BILLOWING MUSLIN

Floaty butter muslin is one of the cheapest ways to cover a large window without blocking out all the light. The fabric here is in two pieces, each one long enough to drape over the rail and down to the floor on both sides. One of the lengths was stamped with a sponge cut-out in the shape of a melon half. The two pieces were hung next to each other and knotted about halfway down. The stamped half crosses over to the other side and so adds rhythm to the draped fabric Take time to arrange the fabric so that enough billows out above the knot and a generous amount spills over the floor as well. The natural look is completed by using bamboo and raffia instead of a traditional rail.

YOU WILL NEED

- ◆ tracing paper
- ◆ pencil
- ◆ thin card, for template
- ◆ block of high-density foam (as used for camping mattresses)
- ◆ craft knife
- ◆ 2 lengths of butter muslin
- ◆ 2 bamboo poles, window width
- ◆ sewing machine (optional)
- ◆ needle and matching sewing thread
- ◆ backing card
- ◆ iron
- ◆ fabric paint: coffee-brown and dark brown
- ◆ plate
- ◆ paint roller or brush
- ◆ tape
- ◆ drill
- ◆ wallplugs and cup hooks
- ◆ bundle of natural coloured raffia

1 Trace the template from the back of the book, enlarging to the required size. Place it on the foam block, then cut around it with a craft knife. Scoop out the inner area, leaving the printing surface intact.

2 Fold both of the muslin lengths in half. Form a channel along the top of each, about 5cm/2in down from the fold. It must be the width of the two bamboo poles as they will slide into it. Sew by machine or hand.

3 Place one piece of the muslin on to the backing card on a work surface. Smooth the muslin out as much as possible – if it has been pre-washed, it will have crinkled up and may need ironing first.

4 Put some of the coffee-brown fabric paint on to the plate and run the roller through it until it is evenly coated. Use the roller to ink the foam stamp.

5 Start stamping the pattern, rotating the stamp in your hand each time you print. Leave more or less the same amount of space between prints, but do not worry about achieving a precise spacing.

6 To add depth and variety to the stamping, mix the dark brown into the coffee-brown, then coat the roller with the new shade and cover the stamp.

7 Stamp the darker prints among the lighter ones in a random way. Fix the fabric paint with a hot iron following the manufacturer's instructions.

8 Temporarily tape over the ends of the bamboo poles so that they don't catch on the loose-woven muslin, and slide the poles through the sewn channels on both curtains. ⟶

9 Drill holes and insert the wallplugs and cup hooks in the top of the window recess, about 10–15cm/4–6in in from the sides. Cut ten 45cm/18in strips of raffia and use five on either side, twisted together into a rope, to bind the bamboo poles together in place of the tape. Use the loose ends to suspend the bamboo rail by tying them to the cup hooks.

10 Tie a knot with the two curtains about halfway down their length. Experiment with different effects, but take your time over the positioning of the knot, its shape and the way the muslin drapes over it.

Above: A twisted branch holds one long length of muslin away from the window, adding interest to the drape.

Right: The window treatment works within a limited range of natural colours, but is made interesting by the fabric drapes and textural variety.

MATERIALS

Throughout this book, a range of imaginative materials has been used to add character to the individual projects. Many of the items are a good deal cheaper than conventional curtain fixings, too.

Creative window dressers have a few key tools in their work box, the first being the staple gun. Staple guns come in a range of sizes and take staples of varying lengths. The smallest is not much good for holding heavy fabric and the largest is for the building trade, so buy one somewhere in the middle.

You also need a hammer, pliers, tape measure, spirit level and electric drill. A screwdriver, bradawl and various pairs of scissors should complete the kit. Hardware stores have interesting fixings, such as garage hooks, plumbing pipe holders and balls of string of every thickness.

Yachting chandlers are another useful point of reference. They are often crammed with cleats, hooks, cables and gadgets for adjusting tension. They go by technical names such as deck-eyes, thimbles and rigging screws.

Right: A selection of materials suitable for hanging, fixing and decorating curtains. Some of these appear in the projects, while others may be used for your own creations.

Stamped muslin (1); thick twisted cord (2); plastic-coated curtain wire (3); sari fabric (4); artificial cherries (5); velcro tape (6); milliner's velvet (7); iron-on hem fix (8); double-sided carpet tape (9); pinking shears (10); long-arm stapler (11); staple gun (12); hessian (13); metal hook (14); vine eye (15); crane snap (16); kilt pin (17); shower rail and socket (18, 19); paperclips (20); bamboo canes (21, 22); dowelling (23); long-nose pliers (24); small bulldog clips (25); cup hook (26); key rings (27); split brass rings (28); solid brass rings (29); hinged document rings (30); iron pipe holders (31); brass eyelets (32); rigging wire (33); steel eyelet (34); rigging screw (35); washing line (36); butcher's hooks (37); garage/chain hook (38); buckled leather straps (39); clothes pegs (40); cotton reel (41); picture rail hooks (42); right-angle bracket (43); plastic-coated cup hooks (44); plastic-coated cleat (45); brass hook (46); brass cleat (47); iron cleat (48); steel cleat (49); crocodile clips (50)

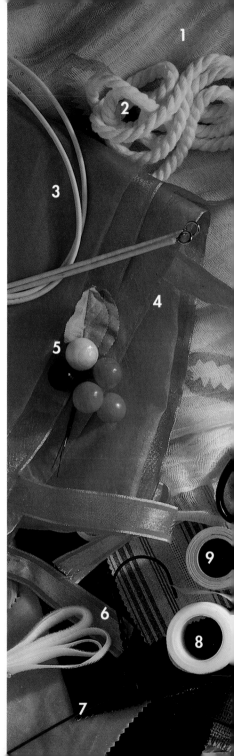

TECHNIQUES

Everybody has their own way of doing

things, but sometimes the "proper" way is

a complete revelation and actually quite

helpful. It has often developed out of

everyone else's hit-and-miss attempts and

although it might seem like stating the

obvious, here are a few basic guidelines to

point you in the right direction.

Fixing a curtain rail

1 To insert a wallplug, you need to match the drill bit number to the size of the wallplug. They are coded, so check the numbers. Hold the wallplug next to the bit, then use a strip of tape to mark its length on the bit. You should not drill deeper than this or you will lose the wallplug in the wall. You need a masonry bit for drilling walls and these can be recognized by their light colour and squared-off tips. Wood drill bits are made of darker metal.

2 Having drilled the hole to the required depth, tap the wallplug in with a hammer. It should fit in snugly right up to the collar. If it is too loose, it is best to fill it and re-locate the fixing hole at least 5cm/2in from it. If the hole is too tight, the wallplug will distort and the fixing will not be secure – check the drill bit and go up one size if necessary.

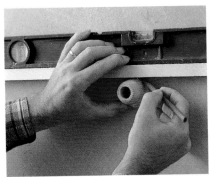

Stapling velcro to a wooden batten

3 A standard wooden curtain rail fitting comes in two parts – the first is a cup shape with a hole drilled through the middle for a screw. The second has a peg that fits into the hole, and a ring at the other end to hold the pole. Measure above the window to get the position for the first support fixing. Drill and plug a hole, then screw the wooden cup in place. Peg the second half of the fitting into it and put in the securing screw through the hole provided.

4 To position the second support fixing, rest a length of plank on the first fixing and place a spirit level on top of it. Hold the wooden cup in your spare hand and when you find the level, mark through the hole with a pencil. You can then dispense with the plank and spirit level. Drill, plug and screw in the fixing as before. Thread the rail through the rings or rest it in the grooves, then push the finials on to the ends to finish off the curtain rail.

Different types of velcro suit different jobs – some have one self-adhesive and one plain edge, while others need stitching or ironing on. Here, you can see a length of velcro being stapled to a batten. This can then be used for attaching pelmets or pleating curtains. A staple gun is indispensable for this kind of strong, instant fixing.

Working with iron-on hem fix

Once you have discovered the ease of ironing up a hem as opposed to sewing it, you just won't look back! The bonding film comes in a roll of varying widths and has the same stiffening effect as interfacing. It is very useful for getting a crisp folded edge, and its added weight also makes fabrics hang better.

Simply put the iron-on hem fix inside the folded seam and press it with an iron. If the fabric is light and delicate, use a cloth between it and the iron to protect the fabric from direct heat.

Pleating with a staple gun

1 Use a length of wooden batten for the pleating – you can fix it to the wall with a couple of strong screws. Start by putting the first staple into the corner of the fabric. Use the staple gun on its side so that the staples are vertical, not horizontal, which would cause more stress on the fabric and possible tearing.

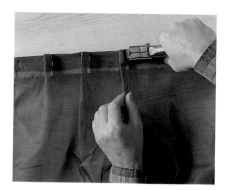

2 Allow an equal distance between pleats, then pinch the same amount each time between your finger and thumb to lift it clear of the batten. Place a staple on each side of the pinched pleat. When you reach the end of the length, go back to the beginning and staple all the pinched pleats down flat in the same direction. If your pelmet is deep, you may prefer to leave out this stage.

CALCULATING FABRIC

The first step to estimating how much fabric to use is to decide what look you are trying to achieve. Most of the projects in this book are not based on conventional approaches to window dressing, so many traditional concerns are irrelevant here. Beach mats, tartan rugs, plastic blinds and garden trellises, to name but a few of the materials used, come in predetermined sizes. You will have to judge for yourself whether your windows are the right proportions to accommodate these treatments. However, when it comes to draping fabrics, whether using conventional methods or the short-cuts described here, there are a few rules to help you decide how much fabric you need. To determine the overall length, measure from the top of the curtain fitting, taking into account the methods for hanging, and the hem allowances, to the floor. If you want a billowed, draped effect, you will need to allow more material to drape on to the floor – anything from 15cm/6in upwards, depending on the look you want. You will also need to measure the width of the window, adding on the amount the curtain fitting extends either side. You will have to increase your measurements according to the fullness required. For fuller curtains you may need fabric 1½ times as wide as the window, but for a blind, you will only need to accommodate the extent of the fittings on either side of the window.

In this treatment, the muslin used was as wide as possible – one piece was the width of the window. Depending on the size of your window you may need to stitch two pieces together. The first curtain spills on to the floor, requiring a length of at least 1¼ x the length of the window. To achieve the drape on the second curtain, a piece 1½ x the length of the window was used.

To estimate the amount of fabric required for a curtain with a pelmet such as this one, measure from the curtain rail to the floor (or less) for the desired length, adding the required hem allowance at either end. The pelmet requires an additional 60cm/24in. You need a total width allowance of approximately 1½ x the width of the window.

This treatment uses two king-size cotton sheets, creating a very full, draped effect. Each "curtain" is wider than the actual window.

For this treatment, you need three equal-size pieces – two for the curtains, and one for the pelmet. For fullness, consider a total fabric width of 1½ x the window.

T E M P L A T E S

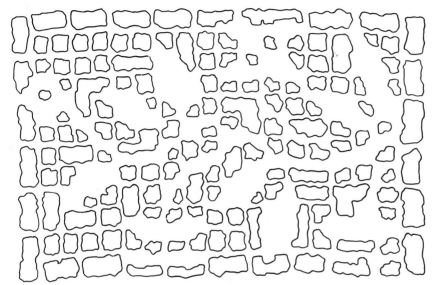

Victorian Stencil design

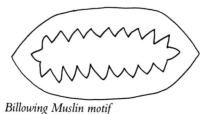

Billowing Muslin motif

ACKNOWLEDGEMENTS

The authors and publishers would like to thank the following for generously supplying materials used in this book:

After Noah
121 Upper Street
London N1 1QP
(furniture and galvanized accessories)

Crown Decorative Products Ltd
P.O. Box 37
Crown House
Hollins Road
Darwen
Lancashire BB3 0BG
(suppliers of paint)

McCloud & Co Limited Decorative
Accessories
269 Wandsworth Bridge Road
London SW6 2TX
(gold furniture on page 31)

Ruffle & Hook
Florence Works
34 ½ Florence Street
London N1 2DT
(curtain fabrics, tassels and curtain poles)

Picture credits
p8 Camera Press; **p9** *bottom* Arcaid © Eric Sierins; *top left* Arcaid; *top right* Arcaid © Richard Waite; **p10** *left* Arcaid © Julie Phipps; *right* Camera Press; **p11** *top left* Elizabeth Whiting Associates; *bottom left and right* Camera Press; **p12** Robert Harding Picture Library; **p13** *top left, top right and bottom left* Camera Press; *bottom right* Elizabeth Whiting Associates; **p14** Robert Harding Picture Library © Tim Beddow; **p15** *left* Robert Harding Picture Library © James Merril; *top right* Habitat PR; *bottom right* Arcaid © Earl Carter, designer: Shane Chandler; **p16** Elizabeth Whiting Associates; **p17** *bottom left* Arcaid © Richard Bryant; *top right* Arcaid © Ray Main; *right* Robert Harding Picture Library

INDEX